King Arthur
——IN SOMERSET——

ROSEMARY CLINCH & MICHAEL WILLIAMS

BOSSINEY BOOKS

First published in 1987
by Bossiney Books
St Teath, Bodmin, Cornwall.
Typeset and printed in Great Britain
by Penwell Ltd,
Parkwood, Callington, Cornwall.

ISBN 0 948158 25 5

PLATE ACKNOWLEDGEMENTS

Front cover: Michael Clinch
Drawings by Paul Honeywill
Rosemary Clinch: Pages 7, 12, 15, 18, 38, 41, 47, 48, 52,
53, 56, 61, 66, 68, 72, 74, 79, 80, 82, 83, 93
Mark Bygrave: 11, 23, 25, 33, 34, 35, 43, 51, 55, 58, 59
62, 63, 64, 86, 89, 90
Michael Clinch: 21, 30, 69, 70, 78
Roy Westlake: back cover
Julia Davey: page 17

About the Authors

Michael Williams, a Cornishman, started full-time publishing in 1975. With his wife Sonia, he runs Bossiney Books from a cottage and converted barn in North Cornwall—they are literally cottage publishers, specializing in Westcountry subjects by Westcountry authors. For ten years they ran the Bossiney House Hotel, just outside Tintagel—hence the name Bossiney Books.

Outside publishing and writing, Michael Williams is a keen cricket enthusiast. He is President of the Cornish Crusaders Cricket Club and a member of the Cornwall and Gloucestershire County Clubs. He is also a member of the RSPCA, and has actively worked for reform in laws relating to animal welfare. In 1984 he was elected to the Ghost Club and remains convinced Cornwall is the most haunted area in Great Britain.

His most recent titles are *The Moors of Cornwall, Paranormal in the Westcountry*, and, as co-author, *Secret Westcountry*.

Rosemary Clinch, who lives near Bristol, is one of Bossiney's most prolific authors. She made her debut for Bossiney in the summer of 1984, contributing a chapter in *Strange Somerset Stories*. Then early in 1985 she was co-author of *Unknown Somerset*, an exploration of off-the-beaten-track places in 'The County of Romantic Splendour'.

Later in 1985 she wrote Bossiney's first Bristol title: *Unknown Bristol*. David Foot, in his perceptive Introduction, reflected: 'I get the firm impression that Rosemary Clinch relishes looking round the corners and under the pavement stones just like I do.' One shrewd reviewer has likened her approach and style to that of the great James Cameron.

In 1986 she contributed *Supernatural in Somerset* to the Bossiney list, a title which immediately won some golden opinions and was featured on BBC Radio Bristol. She is also the subject of a chapter in *Paranormal in the Westcountry* and is one of five authors who have put together *People & Places in Bristol* introduced by bestselling international novelist E.V. Thompson.

More recently Rosemary is co-author of *Secret Westcountry* in which she has gone for the facts and the questions *behind* the stories or the headlines. Currently she is researching a new book on Bristol.

Of her authorship in *King Arthur Country in Somerset*, Michael Williams writes: 'Like that great Westcountry traveller and writer, Lady Clara Vyvyan, Rosemary has the ability to captivate both the eye and the mind . . . she is a real Arthurian student—a seeker *par excellence* . . .'

Contents

King Arthur in Somerset

by Michael Williams

Just occasionally myth triumphs over fact.

Arthur *may* have been no more than a sixth-century chieftain, but his importance lies not in what the man was. His importance is in what he has become. The stories surrounding Arthur and his Court are among the most moving and profound the world has known.

The enigma of Arthur is part of the fascination, and speculation has been with us a long time—as long ago as 1485 when Caxton printed Malory's *Le Morte d'Arthur*. It was Thomas Malory who established Arthur in Camelot, saying it was Winchester. Yet his editor in the Introduction stated Camelot was in Wales.

But we, who live and work in the Westcountry, *feel* Somerset is Camelot, and we shall see how feelings are important to this whole Arthurian quest.

An eccentric well-travelled antiquarian, John Leland of Henry VIII's reign, was the first to 'discover' our Westcountry connection. He came to Somerset and wrote: 'At the very south end of the church of South Cadbury standeth Camelot, sometimes a famous town or castle . . . The people can tell nothing there but that they have heard say that Arthur much resorted to Camelot.'

Leland later went on to describe the nearby village of Queen Camelot, though the final syllable may have been his personal invention. By the 1800s there was a whole range of Arthurian stories linked to Cadbury Castle: Arthur and his knights sleeping in a cave, watering their horses at the well, and riding out from here on their exploits.

Author, Michael Williams, in contemplative mood at Glastonbury Abbey.

Though comparisons can be dangerous—not to say odious—King Arthur and Jesus of Nazareth have an important something in common. There *is* evidence of the historical existence of both, but there are no authentic documents to prove either.

Pascal reflected that, from the point of view of sheer logic, it was not more absurd to believe in the existence of God than not to believe, and we might say something similar of Arthur. Logically it's not more absurd to believe than not to believe that there genuinely *was* a British King, called Arthur, living in the fifth century.

Although some people say the tales surrounding Arthur are purely fiction, it is difficult to account for their enduring quality unless there was a man whose personality and achievements formed the rock on which the battlements and the towers of the legends were built.

Arthur has been a name to conjure with for fifteen centuries. Medieval man was certain Arthur ruled, but scholars in the Age of Reason were sceptical. Gibbon, though, had faith in an historical Arthur, and today more and more seekers consider Arthur a probability rather than a possibility.

Many of the legends portray an illustrious British King or Emperor, a man who conquered most of western Europe, who ruled his dominions from the glittering court of Camelot.

The evidence—if there were such—might have produced a different picture, a different man. But we do know that in the fifth century, the Roman Empire in the west collapsed. Roman control was threatened in Britain with conquest by the Saxons. Around AD 500 the British army won a decisive battle, and it is reasonable to suppose victory came through an inspired, inspiring leader. In that event, Arthur almost certainly grew out of the body and deeds of that leader. The terrible irony is that this great British hero fought against the ancestors of the modern Britons. Irony deepens too in that Arthur was almost certainly not a King but a British aristocrat, partly Roman, partly Celtic. Artorius was his Roman surname—which is thought to be a Latinised form of a Celtic name meaning 'bear'. There is a suggestion that he led cavalry, and out of

Paul Honeywill captures the powerful supernatural quality of Merlin.

his horsemanship and leadership grew the mounted knights of the medieval legends.

All of which brings us to the important question: can there truly be such a thing as pure myth?

For centuries men and women have been telling stories about Arthur. From ancient legends and scraps of half-forgotten history, a great epic has been forged, helping to shape music and literature, sparking ideas and ideals. Yet some scholars dismiss it all as a figment of fertile Celtic imagination.

One man who does not is author Colin Wilson. Writing in *King Arthur Country in Cornwall*, he answered the sceptics with conviction:

'Commonsense tells us that there is no smoke without fire. The other legendary king of romance is Charlemagne, and we know he existed, because he made his mark all over Europe, and there are hundreds of records. Arthur was an obscure British general who lived three hundred years before Charlemagne, in a remote corner of the then-known civilised world, and there are no contemporary records, unless, as is likely, the references in Nennius are quotations from such documents. But the spread of his fame from Wales to England then across Europe, suggests that he was a real person. In fact, I find it difficult to call to mind any famous mythical figure who was absolute and pure invention; even Dr Faustus really existed.'

In that same book, Colin Wilson, who has lived in Cornwall for a quarter of a century, pondered on the implications after Arthur's death, coming to this conclusion:

'With Arthur dead, the Saxons again burst out of Kent. With no great leader to unite them, the divided local chieftains were defeated one at a time. Within ten years of his death, the surviving chiefs must have realised that his overthrow was the end of an era—and one of the greatest tragedies to befall the British nation. Twenty years after that, the Saxons marched into Glastonbury. Fortunately, Arthur's grave was unmarked; but the tradition of its existence continued to survive in Wales and Cornwall, where the Celts had retreated in the face of the invader.

Dunster Castle today: '. . . visible sites to fire the imagination.'

To Glastonbury over Mendip—seeing changes
in the landscape in the light of the legend.

'But although this new Angle-land had forgotten Arthur, the Celtic
bards remembered him. The legends and poems proliferated. And
Arthur's real conquest—the conquest of the European imagination—began.'

Despite modern education, the emphasis on science, it is a curious
fact that a high percentage of people today remain superstitious.
Julie Welch, whose perceptive journalism graces the pages of *The
Observer*, has reflected: 'Even among some of the well-known people
I talked to, there is a feeling that the world is a pretty terrible place
at the moment—that superstition is the panacea against its
hideousness . . . successful people, whom you would think would be
the last to need such reassurance.'

In such a climate, it is not surprising there is need for a hero like
Arthur. There is a Supernatural parallel here—I think so anyway.
Though the Supernatural has not yet qualified as a science, there
are certain Supernatural facts which must make the scientist
uneasy. Likewise Arthur. If Arthur did not exist, then there would

have been a compulsion to invent him. That, at least, is the view of a Cornishman who lives near Tintagel, where some say Arthur was born.

Though this is essentially a journey among the Arthurian sites in Somerset and Avon, some reference to Tintagel in North Cornwall is necessary. It was at Tintagel 21 years ago that my interest in Arthur was born, and I was lucky in that first summer in North Cornwall to come across a single sentence from that controversial cleric, Father Bernard Walke. 'I do not know what historical evidence there is concerning Tintagel and the Holy Grail legend, but I am convinced that something of spiritual import happened here.' That is not only true of Tintagel, but of many of the sites explored in Somerset and Avon. You *feel* something important happened *here*.

You have only to stand on the cliffs at Tintagel on a fine summer's evening, when the sun slopes westward beyond the Atlantic 'from

Dolebury—it is a place where we can believe Arthur lived.

something like a flaming battlefield' to believe in Arthur. And it is a matter of belief; Cornwall, Somerset, the whole world in fact, have consciously willed the legends to be true.

It is to Tintagel that we come for the birth of Arthur—and there are two versions. Geoffrey of Monmouth, with great imagination, saw this dramatic fortress on a magical stretch of Westcountry coastline as the birthplace for Arthur: a good choice. We must remember that this Welsh Bishop, back in the twelfth century, wrote to satisfy a thirst for romance, bravery and chivalry all those years ago, and if he were able to travel on some time machine, forward into the last quarter of the twentieth century, he would be intrigued to find the same thirst living on.

Geoffrey of Monmouth's story of the birth went like this:

Uther Pendragon, King of Britain, became infatuated with Ygraine, wife of Gorlois, Duke of Cornwall, rated the most beautiful woman in the kingdom. The King's interest in her was such that her husband kept her virtually a prisoner at Tintagel. Infuriated, Uther descended on Cornwall. Such was his longing for the woman that Merlin, the Wizard, prescribed a magic brew enabling him to look like the twin brother of Gorlois. Thus disguised, he had no difficulty in entering the Castle and that night he slept with Ygraine. As a result Arthur was conceived. Gorlois was defeated and killed in battle with Uther's army, and his wife, now liberated, became Queen of Britain.

The second version of Arthur's birth is charged with magic and Supernatural powers. Some writers have even suggested Arthur was conceived of the Gods. Again if you stand on the cliffs at Tintagel on a stormy day, with an angry Atlantic climbing the walls of the cliffs, you can, in the eye of your imagination, picture Merlin's acceptance of the babe from the ocean.

Whichever version we accept, Merlin will always live on at Tintagel, for directly below the ruins is Merlin's Cave. Full of atmosphere and drama, it is a magical cave cutting right through to a small rocky beach on the other side of the headland. It is interesting to reflect that Cornwall is often known as the Land of Merlin, and we cannot begin to understand Arthur until we know

Archaeologists name this hillfort Cadbury-Congresbury.

Merlin and appreciate his influence on Arthur, the boy and King.

Tintagel apart, this is a journey across the varied and beautiful acres of Somerset and Avon, and we can have no better guide and companion than Rosemary Clinch.

I first travelled with Rosemary as co-author in 1985 when we put together *Unknown Somerset*. On that occasion, I wrote: 'Thanks to Rosemary, I now find myself travelling across the county with a deeper insight and understanding, a sharper sense of anticipation. Her wanderings conceal real art, careful planning and intuition.' And it is those very qualities which encouraged me to ask her to collaborate on this Arthurian quest.

She is not only a perceptive traveller, she feels a special attunement with Somerset. In her recently published *Supernatural in Somerset* Rosemary admitted: 'Somerset has always had some special kind of magic for me.' Moreover she can catch tone and tempo, and has that rare gift of sharing experience. In her writing, on her journeys—be they physically in the present or in her imagination—one can enjoy the feeling that we are making them too. Like that great Westcountry traveller and writer, Lady Clara Vyvyan, Rosemary has the ability to captivate both the eye and the mind.

Outside and beyond all this, she is a real Arthurian student—a seeker *par excellence* in fact. Again, like Lady Vyvyan, she has an adventurous spirit, an observant mind. All these qualities, then, make her the perfect guide and companion for an Arthurian quest such as ours.

Modern writers and the media have made the anti-hero fashionable, but Arthur goes against that trend. He looks and reads like the traditional hero. Born of the ruling class, skilful and gracious, courageous and honourable, painters and illustrators have tended to depict him as gentlemanly, aristocratic. It is interesting that strong actors like Richard Burton and Richard Harris have played the Arthur role.

Arthur is a finely balanced character. A formidable fighter but not a brute. But maybe that is us: we clothe him with superhuman characteristics. We want our hero to rise above ordinary levels of

The tower on Glastonbury Tor: '. . . the remnants of a strong magic . . .'

17

The waters of the River Brue would have
spread in a wide lake over the marshes in
Arthur's time leading to the local view that it
was here that the King threw his sword
Excalibur.

courage and strength. Richard Cavendish in his fine book *King
Arthur & The Grail* comments on this important heroic theme:

'He needs the gentler qualities and a nobler purpose than to kill
for the love of killing, or to acquire power and wealth. He is loyal to
a leader, to people for whom he is responsible, to an ideal. A king's
bodyguard defends him to the death. David risks his life against the
giant Goliath to protect the Israelites. Beowulf is killed saving his
people from a monstrous dragon.

'The hero's guiding star is his ideal of what he ought to be.'

It is tempting, perhaps inevitable, to start searching for the 'real' Arthur, by peeling away the romantic veneer. The trouble is that stripping away the myths, the veneer, one risks the danger of unwrapping the huge 'present' that is really one carefully wrapped box inside another—and another—until one ends up with a small empty box!

The study of how and why legends live on—and sometimes change emphasis—is interesting. Sally Jones in her thoughtful *Legends of Somerset*, has said: 'The legends of Somerset are like a game of "Chinese Whispers" played long ago . . . Over the years, the stories gradually acquire a deeper resonance as the echoes of the original event, far from dying down, continue to rumble and reverberate.'

Sally in that same Bossiney title explored the possible reasons why some places retain an atmosphere of the past.

'It seems from hundreds of testimonies and eye-witness accounts that the Battle of Sedgemoor has in some way produced a ripple in the ether, as if the high emotion, the pain and desperation surrounding it, have imprinted themselves on the places where the tragic events were played out.

'Just as at the scores of sites like Edge Hill and Glencoe a tangible sense of terror remains and the sights and sounds of battle recur as if the whole event was being re-run time and again over the centuries on a hazy and faintly out-of-focus projector. Many of the people living near Sedgemoor accept as a matter of fact that, from time to time, they hear the hooves of a troop of 'King' Monmouth's men cantering along an ancient track en route to the slaughter.

'Such experiences seem most accessible to psychics and those sympathetic to another world and it is easy to dismiss them as the working of a well-informed imagination or the effect of drifting shapes produced by marshland mist. All the same, the fact that so many solid non-believers with no previous knowledge of the battle have yet been granted a "ringside seat" suggests there is far more to the accounts than this.

'. . . It is as if some spiritual tremor has shivered down the ages and made itself felt where the veil is thinnest . . .'

All of which brings me back briefly to Tintagel. Peter Underwood, President of the Ghost Club and a fellow Bossiney author, assures me there have been reported glimpses of Arthur's ghost among the ruins of the Castle of Tintagel.

I happen to believe the case for ghosts is so overwhelming it scarcely warrants any form of *intelligent* opposition. The thousands and thousands of sightings cannot all be the vision of the neurotic or the charlatan. In my researches into the subject, I have interviewed more than two hundred people, and some of them are—or were—very down-to-earth types.

So, if we accept that the ghost of Arthur has been seen at Tintagel, we must therefore presume, reasonably enough, that Arthur once lived.

A few years ago Fate kindly put me on a particular path, and it is quite possible I have, in fact, met the 'real' Arthur. That path is called psycho-expansion. This technique allows people to explore and develop their sense of awareness, a technique which enables the mind to move in time and space. Personally I have not undergone psycho-expansion, but I have interviewed people in the state of regression—travelling back in time. Those critics who cannot accept reincarnation, will be unable to accept psycho-expansion because the subject, in regressing, goes back to a former life or lives—some say they also have the ability to go forward in time and can therefore tell us what lies in the thing we call the future.

The most remarkable claim inside Barney Camfield's group is that one member *was* King Arthur in a former life. A Westcountry housewife with brown eyes, I have interviewed her twice. On both occasions she regressed to Arthur's time. She sees nothing strange or inconsistent in that once she was a man. 'Some people come back to this life many times,' she explained, 'and in very different forms . . . there seem to be no rules, save those of cause and effect.'

She went on to explain: 'Arthur had this great charisma. But he wasn't the chivalrous character that some of the story-tellers would have us believe. As a young man he was keen on women and fathered as many as fifteen children in various parts of Britain by various women.'

Within moments rather than minutes, she appeared to sink into a trance—the average layman watching her move from 'now' to 'then' would probably call it 'self-hypnosis'. In this condition her voice

A bridge over the River Cam—was this the site of the Battle of Camlann?

becomes noticeably lower in key, assuming an intensity that was not there earlier.

During both interviews I was forced to one of two conclusions: either this Aquarian lady was a convincing actress or I was watching and listening to something quite out of this world. At times, she appeared troubled, and at other times amused. Hers was no matter-of-fact commentary, no plateau of emotion or response to events.

In each interview she came out of a seemingly sleeping state gradually, just like someone awakening from a deep sleep or a dream, giving the impression of a weary traveller, arriving at a destination, or getting back. Barney Camfield describes the condition as 'relaxation of the mind . . . then comes what was termed by Goethe "contemplative perception".'

It was in our second conversation that we concentrated on the Somerset aspects of the Arthurian story. We talked on a wild March day, when rain and high winds swept across the landscape. Yet within a matter of moments, my visitor was back in another time and place. As soon as she had slipped into a state of psycho-expansion, I asked her: 'Did Arthur really have a Somerset link?'

'Now the thing to think of', she said, 'is the whole of the south-west peninsula, and that this man operated in that area . . . the link with Somerset is strong. I am pulled back in the experiences I have to the Glastonbury area, and to south of that area, into Dorset in fact, which was where I believe I was born. But Glastonbury in the years running up to 500 AD had a very, very strong power, the earth power if you like, a ley line, a meeting of leys and it looked like a grid if you were able to see it: grids of light . . . there are one or two very strong ones which go running right through the Tor. In the present day you can still feel them but they are overlaid with many other centuries of happenings.'

Rosemary Clinch will, in fact, be putting further questions to this lady who was Arthur on her part of the journey.

Before leaving the subject of psycho-expansion, I was interested to learn from the man who was Merlin that Merlin 'acted as a Kissinger type and got the tribes together'.

> **Arthur's grave at Glastonbury—was it a twelfth-century publicity stunt?**

Morgana also confirmed the Somerset link. This is what she told me: 'Born 478 AD at a Roman type villa near Old Sarum, about one and a half miles away from the present day Salisbury in Wiltshire. Dressed in Roman style and lived in a Roman type villa.

'Half sister to Arthur—same Mother. Met Merlin when I was about eight years old. He came to the villa looking for me. Later took me away and taught me all the things I would need to know. I had a stone circle that I used a lot just to the north of the villa.

'Later used Glastonbury Tor. Temple built there, with stone circle around it. Inside magnificent mosaic floor, set out with twelve pointed star, each point lining up with the stone column outside. The twelve signs of the zodiac were set between each point of the star. This Temple was used to give Arthur a spiritual boost when needed. I had six other helpers. At one time we sat cross-legged on the floor and tried to hold back the enemy with thought power.

'After Arthur's last battle which was some sort of civil war he was killed and I fled to Glastonbury with the crystal in the gold bowl. Percival was with me. We hid the crystal in the rock which we could open and close with thought power. Then we fled into Wales where I died in 512 AD.'

So we have these interesting strands linking Somerset to Arthur—indeed the Westcountry as a whole seems to feature significantly. The cynics, of course, will snort derision about these psycho-expansionists. But it is worth reminding them that Dr Arthur Guirdham, a respected British physician, is convinced he is a reincarnated member of a thirteenth-century religious sect, about which he has written with considerable accuracy and detail.

Why not Barney Camfield's Arthurian set then?

The Westcountry is Arthur's traditional homeland. Other parts of Britain—indeed other countries overseas have claimed him—but the most probing of historians have been unable to uproot him conclusively from Somerset and Cornwall.

The big reason for locating Arthur here is that he is accepted as the conquering hero of the Battle of Badon, when the Britons scored a sensational victory over the Saxons. The precise location of Mt Badon remains a tantalizing puzzle but most historians, pressed to make a decision, would say it was somewhere in the South West.

Despite the reservations of some of them, there has been a massive ongoing tradition firmly establishing Arthur in the Westcountry in popular opinion. Though Geoffrey of Monmouth is

Dunster — '. . . dramatic Arthur country.'

accused of invention when he puts Tintagel as Arthur's birthplace and Bath the scene of the Battle of Badon, it is feasible to assume the Welsh writer kept his ears open for the folklore and the poems with Arthurian reference. The infuriating thing—or maybe the magic of it all—is so little was written down. Consequently we shall never know where traditional beliefs came to a stop and Geoffrey's vivid imagination took over.

This then is a journey among the various Arthurian sites in Somerset and Avon.

Arthur, in a very real sense, belongs to these varied westerly landscapes. Indeed, we begin to see these territories in a different light when we explore them in the shadow of Arthur. Therefore, does it really matter whether these Arthurian links are genuine history or folk tales? We think it is more important to regard them as something creative, a combination of ancient memory and invention.

There may be no assured grave of the King, but burial places of the famous can produce curious experiences. We can stand by Sir Winston Churchill's grave in the heart of the green Oxfordshire

countryside—and somehow be strengthened. Yet Sir Winston is both there and not there.

So Arthur's ability to live on—and he does live on—may be fortified oddly enough by the fact there is no final earthly resting place—for certainty that is.

It is interesting how Arthur has worked on a whole succession of writers. Thomas Malory, a great writer, Geoffrey of Monmouth, an imaginative one, Alfred Tennyson, whose *Idylls of the King* are among the greatest versions of the legends, and T.H. White, author of *The Once and Future King*, are only some who have been fired and inspired by the Arthurian theme.

Each succeeding writer has added his or her embellishments, but in the opinion of many good literary judges, *Morte d'Arthur* stands supreme. Malory, giving purpose and form to the old tales, made Arthur and his knights living characters—after the pattern and style of his time.

They were curious times—those uncertain days of the Wars of the Roses—and yet full of promise, for this was the springtime of modern English. The love of Lancelot for Guinevere, the Quest for the Holy Grail, the fellowship of the Round Table, the treason of Mordred—Malory handled such themes powerfully, crafting—some say—the earliest novel in our language.

Then there were the Pre-Raphaelite painters, talented painters like Sir Edward Burne-Jones and Dante Gabriel Rossetti, working on Arthurian characters and Arthurian scenes, inspired by the writings of Tennyson and Malory.

The Lady of Shalott by J.W. Waterhouse, with her long strands of tawny hair and pensive face as her craft glides through the water, and Morgan le Fay, the beautiful but wicked half-sister, an enchantress who smashed the Round Table and its knights, by Frederick Sandys, are just two beautiful paintings from this school.

The Victorian era was, in fact, an important watershed in Arthurian matters. W.H. Auden may have called Tennyson the man

'The Lady of Shalott . . . with her long strands of tawny hair and pensive face as her craft glides through the water.'

who 'had the finest ear, perhaps, of any English poet; he was also undoubtedly the stupidist' but the fact remains Tennyson breathed great vitality into the whole Arthurian romance. 'Poetry', as he once reflected, 'is shot-silk, with many glancing colours. Every reader must find his own interpretation according to his ability, and according to his sympathy with the poet.

'The power of romance is that it fits itself anew to every period. Each one takes up again the undying legend of Arthur and more or less deludes itself with the notion that the latest version is the truest. But every century must still read its own emotion, and its own colours into the past.'

Those words were written more than eighty years ago and still have a true and relevant ring.

Nowhere are these Arthurian stories brought to life more vividly—or sustained—than here in Somerset and Avon. Man-made constructions and landscapes dating from a distant past all combine to produce the quintessential Arthurian character—and quality.

'Arthur lives on . . .' That is the feeling you get as Rosemary Clinch takes us from place to place.

Moreover, on such a journey we, ourselves, may change, for Arthur has always embodied the highest, the best aims of the human spirit, and many of his battles against the Saxon invaders are symbolic of our own battles in life.

The search for the Holy Grail is, in fact, our inner journey.

In our Cornish version, *King Arthur Country in Cornwall*, co-author and Bossiney editor Brenda Duxbury recalled the magic of the atmosphere of Scilly, those island outposts, a Cornish contender for Avalon, when she reflected:

'When you have left behind the pressures and demands of everyday life—that grosser living that takes so much of our time—and in your search arrive at these final outposts, there you have to stay, for there is no place beyond. And as you fall under the spell of these islands, you realise more and more that now there is no other place to search for the Holy Grail—all our problems have to be resolved within ourselves.'

Somerset is a legend-laden land—Avon, too, despite its recent man-made boundaries. In addition to an Arthurian tour such as ours, you can make a Christian pilgrimage or a Monmouth itinerary. There is undoubtedly a strong, strange haunting quality about this region. Many serious Supernatural claims have been made. Ghostly manifestations at the county museum in Taunton—a curator there believed he was clutched by a pair of ghostly hands and on another occasion saw a blonde young woman in seventeenth-century dress; and at Stogumber they say the Wild Hunt rides through the streets—trotting horses, jingling bridles and baying hounds—some residents say it came through in 1960 but nobody dared look out of the window! These are just two examples of eerie settings.

For years at Creech Hill locals 'in the know' thought it wise to take a lantern and staff when they travelled that way at night in case they encountered a tall ghostly figure with a hideous laugh.

There are wells, too, with healing properties. At Withan Friary St Dunstan's well had a great reputation for curing epilepsy and at Doulting there were two wells with strange powers. At St Aldhelm's the Saint would sit reading the psalms as sick animals were restored, and at St Agnes' Fountain, countrymen brought ailing cattle in the belief they would be restored 'as long as they were not stolen'.

None of this may directly relate to Arthur, but in such a setting, charged with Supernatural undertones, we can see how Arthur fits naturally into the landscape.

Queen Camel, Dunster, Arthur's Bridge, Glastonbury are just some of the sites to which we travel with Rosemary. The very names quicken the imagination—fire speculation.

We firmly believe the Arthurian stories will continue—future generations of writers and film makers will cherish them, yet, at the same time, remoulding, reshaping to meet the needs of a new age and different thinking.

That way Arthur will ride on.

Moreover, as we travel with Rosemary, we shall be discovering the Land of Arthur is still very alive today.

As long as that fact remains, Arthur will never die.

The Arthurian Sites in Somerset

by Rosemary Clinch

Arthur's Somerset

Glastonbury has long been associated with Arthur, the supreme site with its images of an Arthurian Avalon, but we can discover him in many corners of Somerset. Man or myth, king or resistance fighter, he emerges from a sixth-century dark age through an ancient legacy of legend and the chroniclers of history and romance. We can see the sites of modern 'Quests', the search for the Truth, where some dig with the trowel for tangible clues, while others, the unorthodox, the neo-mystic, look to the heavens and on into the mysteries of the cosmos.

We can sample the essential magic of Somerset in the variety of its shape and mood and see why the Saxons, eager for its rich beauty, made it their 'Summer Land'. It is a county where sea shore gives way to vast moorland, where rivers and ribbon-like rhines, pronounced 'reens', are surrounded by dignified and magically-shaped hills. Beyond lie gentler undulations with secret hollows and rich meadows. Nature's design with so many facets has tantalised the minds of writers for centuries. Somerset is *all* things. It defies any single description. In a sense it is like Arthur, containing many elements in its make-up, entrapping the pilgrim into an orbit of exciting, even near-supernatural discoveries. It was a prize for which the *Somersaetas*—as the Saxons were called—had to strive long and hard against the might of Arthur and the strength of a Celtic Westcountry held fast in its traditional roots.

Author Rosemary Clinch.

Fact or fiction, Arthur's command in Somerset would have been vital, a strategic stand in defence of the Westcountry. The sites of battles are long covered in the natural healing of the land, yet some people may sense in the atmosphere the echo of past triumphs or tragedies. The mighty shadow of King Arthur still rules over Somerset, enriching a unique countryside which never ceases to delight and excite the romantic. On our journey we cannot escape his dual personality: a hero both of fancy and reality. They merge along with the familiar stories into the landscape. This is the powerful nature of 'Summer Land' where we can believe Arthur still lives.

South Cadbury Castle—Camelot?

We begin our journey in South Somerset, an area rich in Arthurian folklore, where close to the Dorset border we can see an impressive hill crowned by a hillfort, one of the finest in the county. It is South Cadbury Castle, the tantalising dream of Arthur's Court—Camelot.

There is no doubting the kingly appearance of this ancient hill, five hundred feet in height, for the massive ramparts of the Iron-Age hillfort heave themselves above the thickly wooded slopes. They dominate the little village of South Cadbury below, where near the church we find the rough stoney path of Arthur's Lane with its scattered cowpats. Here we begin our gradual climb, the lane giving way to a more uneven track, soft with the mulch of mud and leaves. Thick, overhanging trees on either side lean their trunks curiously inwards from their banks as if drawn magnetically together by some hidden force. High above, their boughs intermingle to form dark green vaulting and an impression of some grand primaeval aisle. Eventually the trees open, revealing the large grassy plateau of the hill surrounded by an undulating rampart and breath-taking view. On a clear day the searching eye has full command of the hills and vales in the Somerset landscape with Glastonbury Tor rising mystically from its midst.

**To Camelot from South Cadbury. Castle Lane
known by some as Arthur's Lane.**

Leland, the antiquary, may have pronounced in 1542 that
Cadbury Castle is Camelot, but we can conjecture that this belief
had long existed in local lore. If we consider it was here Arthur had
his headquarters, then Somerset can be firmly placed as an
important central point in Arthurian legend but, as the excavations
of the fortification show, not arrayed in all the trappings of a
glittering medieval age.

We can imagine the excitement of archaeologists who in the search
for a real Arthur excavated rich and significant finds on the hill in
the sixties, for the ramparts revealed that during the dark days of

Cadbury Castle: '. . . the tantalising dream of
Arthur's Court—Camelot', and (right) the pathway up to the hillfort is 'like some primaeval
aisle'.

an Arthurian age the hill was re-fortified. Completely encircling the
summit, was a grand structure of stone walls and a wooden
platform for soldiers to walk on, confirming that around Arthur's
time the hill was a stronghold of a great and resourceful chieftain.

On the higher ground of the summit, known for many years as
Arthur's Palace, the foundations of a large building of the
Arthurian period were revealed, a feasting hall constructed of
timber. The remains of a gatehouse and cobbled road at a break in
the ramparts were also found. Through this opening, legend says,
the ghosts of Arthur and his men ride and once a silver horseshoe
was found on the track. If one has the nerve to keep vigil on a night
of the full moon, flickering lights and the glint of hooves might be
seen.

These finds and others of Roman influence have placed South

Cadbury Castle firmly in front of other contenders for the title of Camelot.

Who were the people who used Arthur's Well which lies on the eastern slopes and is said to have magical powers? Maybe, as they drew water, they heard an echo from within of those using Queen Anne's Well higher up the hill. Belief in the hill being hollow may not be all fantasy, but we can wonder at the age-old legend of an iron or golden gate which may open in the hillside showing Arthur asleep in a cave.

As we trace the ramparts of Cadbury Castle, we become consciously aware of how the exploits of Arthur have been indelibly printed into our history, attaching themselves to numerous places in the British countryside. Many are the versions of the tales, penned from a blend of fact and fantasy. We remember how Arthur was born at Tintagel Castle in Cornwall, the son of Ygraine and Uther Pendragon, King of England. Many are the stories of Merlin, the ancient enchanter, who with his magical influence shapes Arthur's earlier years. We hear of the sword in the stone in London which only Arthur can retrieve as the rightful King of England. When it is broken, Merlin replaces it with the mystical sword, Excalibur, which Arthur receives from the Lady of the Lake.

Central to the stories are the symbolic elements. The Round Table represents fellowship and equality, where no man can consider himself of higher status than another. Yet it holds one seat, the Siege Perilous, which only the bravest of knights can occupy, the knight destined to succeed in the Quest of the Holy Grail. A vision in white samite, the Holy Grail appears at Pentecost on the table, before mysteriously vanishing to become the elusive goal of spiritual adventures. The Round Table is also seen as the Grail Table, symbolic of the table of the Last Supper where the 'Dangerous Seat' can be interpreted as the place for the treacherous Judas Iscariot.

It is easy to imagine Arthur coming to Cadbury Castle and marrying the beautiful Guinevere. If the Great Hall found here once witnessed the marriage feast of Arthur and his bride, then it also

Only Arthur, as the rightful king, can pull the sword from the stone.

witnessed the planning for love and war, chivalry and romance against the backdrop of a harder existence. We can still be excited at the words written in the twelfth century by Geoffrey of Monmouth when he says the ladies of the court 'would not deign to have the love of any till he had thrice proved himself in the wars. Wherefore did the ladies wax chaste, and knights the nobler for their love.' As we know, Arthur's most courtly knight, Lancelot, and his Queen Guinevere shared a forbidden love, kept secretly and appeased only by the company they shared in Lancelot's duties for the protection of the Queen. Did this place once witness the trauma of the now familiar 'eternal triangle' as a man, sick in his heart, paced its ramparts?

Was it also here, during the marriage feast, that the Damsel of the Lake enticed Merlin away to finally entomb him in a cave, thereby depriving Arthur of his wise and supernatural counsellor? And did this Camelot see the mischief-making of Morgan le Fay, Arthur's half-sister? She never found the opportunity to steal Excalibur but,

Sutton Montis looking to Cadbury Castle hill.

in her hatred for Arthur, she did manage to unbuckle the magic scabbard and fling it into a deep lake. Wonderful was the sword, for it protected Arthur from losing blood, and without it he was no longer safe from his wounds. These stories tell of broken commandments, but there are also many examples of kindness and love, valour and devotion to duty, stoic attributes which all people admire. They can be seen as the stirrings in a distant past of order, truth and justice in a developing society.

From prehistoric times to the thirteenth century, this noble hill had defended and accommodated its people. It was Iron-Age man who struggled with the mighty task of building the ramparts which supported the great fortress of an Arthurian age. Here can be seen the magnificent labours of men through time, who created for today, the image of a British Troy. No wonder we can believe this was Camelot: from within its walls would have come the sounds of feasting or the fervent planning of battle. Perhaps we *can* hear the echoes of familiar words, as from among valiant men seated at a round table, the voice of one is heard to say to a gathered audience:

> *Behold, for these have sworn*
> *To wage my wars, and worship me their King;*
> *The old order changeth, yielding place to new;*
> *And we that fight for our fair father Christ,*
> *Seeing that ye be grown too weak and old*
> *To drive the heathen from your Roman wall,*
> *No tribute will we pay;*

Idylls of the King

Sutton Montis

To the south-west of Cadbury Castle there is another unnamed and little used pathway which leads downwards towards the village of Sutton Montis. Looking down the steep slope of the ramparts it would seem difficult for a horse and rider to descend this path, yet they did according to local lore. For here, too, the ghosts of Arthur

On Christmas Eve the ghosts of Arthur and his
men are seen slowly descending the ramparts
riding towards Sutton Montis Church.

and his men are seen slowly descending the ramparts on Christmas Eve to ride through the village towards Sutton Montis Church. After watering their horses at a well, which is now hidden in the grounds of Abbey House near the church, they continue on their way with the sound of hooves and the jingle of bridles. In the quiet of the winding narrow lane we can hear the trickle of spring waters coursing through the dense undergrowth bordering the roadside.

We can wonder where Arthur was going, as he rode through Sutton Montis, or what mission he was on. Looking up to Cadbury Castle from the peace of the village, we can consider how whole townships once thrived within the ramparts of the hill, safe, guarded and prepared for the ravages of a hostile existence we do not now experience. Yet, despite our 'land of milk and honey' we suffer a creeping and increasing hostility of greed and assault within our own kind, from which garden wall or fence can do little to protect us. We live vulnerably, spread across the land, forgetful of the needs of society and absorbed in material things. The threat of invasion is always with us and we look to our leaders for a hero who embodies all the attributes that can produce a solution for everlasting peace. Has the spread of Christianity not been enough? Perhaps we need something tangible to accompany a spiritual awareness. As we view the powerful shape of the hill, we can visualise the strong and formidable figure of Arthur and find ourselves agreeing with Brenda Duxbury and Michael Williams when they say in *King Arthur Country in Cornwall*:

'Maybe in looking at Arthur we are looking at society's needs—our own needs—we want *our* hero to rise above ordinary realms of courage, character and physical strength. We clothe him with super-human characteristics.

'We need an Arthur, for Arthur, the hero, brings a special something that our society—and probably most societies outside religious orders—lacks. He brings a something that regenerates Life itself. He makes day-to-day living vivid, purposeful—and worth-

40

while. In history and in fiction—and the line dividing the two is probably thinner and more blurred than we sometimes imagine—the hero offers us a more complete Life.'

River Cam—Camlann?

The River Cam winds its crooked way through the meadows near Cadbury Castle. Though its banks are peaceful now, we know for certain they have witnessed tragedy for in a field called Westwoods, west of the hill, numerous skeletons have been found in trenches. Some have believed these to be the remains of men killed in Arthur's final conflict, the Battle of Camlann.

Rivers have an essential tranquillity. Cool, clear waters course over waving fronds of weed and, on the banks, lush vegetation thrives. Sometimes we hear the sound of a pebble tumbling along the river bed, a reminder of the power the water holds. What once was secure has been uprooted to travel to another resting place. So it was for Arthur at the Battle of Camlann, which may have taken place beside this river.

Deep passions of human nature surface in the many stories of conquest and tragedy. None was more fervent than the jealousy and hatred held for Arthur by his nephew Mordred. Greedy for the Crown of England, he hoped to benefit from the banishment of the valiant Lancelot, and even from the cunning of his mother, Morgan le Fay, when she stole the scabbard to Excalibur which left Arthur so vulnerable. The grim reality of a bitter struggle in these green peaceful fields is a far from pleasant reflection. So terrible was the fight—many good knights lay dead except for Lucan and Bedivere. Arthur had killed Mordred but the traitor had gathered enough

The Battle of Camlann may have taken place beside this now tranquil river.

strength from his wickedness to strike the blow which cleft Arthur's helmet, giving him a frightful wound. The time had come for Arthur to make his final journey.

Merlin's prophecy came true for Arthur, 'that Guinevere was not wholesome for him to take for wife.' We can see in the many versions of the stories how a powerful female element influences the lives of central figures. More dangerous than the male, the women beguile and lie and practise infidelity. At other times we see them more benevolent. Morgan is sinister in Malory but divine in Geoffrey. Even Merlin is fooled in his ill-fated wisdom by the Damsel of the Lake. Tristan and Iseult, with Tristan's Breton wife, and Guinevere and Lancelot, with the Fair Maid of Astolat, share passions with the tragedy of being scorned in love. But it was Guinevere who Mordred took advantage of, causing a division within Arthur's strong government. Political stirrings and the revelation of the Queen's unfaithfulness, resulted in Lancelot's departure with some of the knights to his castle 'Joyous Gard'.

The Round Table was breached, destroying the vital strength of fellowship, the key to Arthur's success in rule. The outcome was inevitable. But Malory gives us hope when he says: 'Yet some men say in many parts of England that King Arthur is not dead, but had by the will of Our Lord Jesu gone into another place; and men say that he shall come again . . .'

Queen Camel

It was not Queen Guinevere who gave the old village, once called just plain Camel, its title. It was Queen Eleanor, wife of King Edward I, for she owned the estate in the thirteenth century. Both King and Queen witnessed a vital part of the Arthurian story, one

Morgan le Fay, Arthur's half sister, mischief-maker of Camelot.

44

Queen Camel—the packhorse bridge over the
River Cam. Does its name link it to Camelot?

which many an historian of today would wish to have seen. In 1278
they watched as the remains of Arthur and Guinevere, found at
Glastonbury, were placed in wooden chests to be buried with all
pomp and ceremony in front of the high altar of the Abbey.

It is the name Camel which has added to the evidence for Cadbury
Castle being the site of Camelot. The finds from the hill tell only half
the story of an Arthurian age. The other half continues to remain an
enigma along with the search for Arthur as a real person. While
many of the indoctrinated hold on to their youthful visions of a
colourful, traditional romance, the more serious grope in the
darkness, searching among the historic fragments of reality,
spurred on by a different kind of charisma.

Wandering around Queen Camel with its tiny packhorse bridge
over the River Cam, we ask, 'What's in a name?' Fanciful notions
are easy and sometimes fun, yet so easily become the seeds of the
stuff of legend. Guinevere was the daughter of King Cameliard and
the implications are tempting. Could the King have given Arthur
and Guinevere Cadbury Castle along with the Round Table as a
wedding present? We hear of Merlin making the Round Table for
Arthur's father Uther, who gives it to Guinevere's father before it
was passed on to Arthur. There was an obvious close and trusting
friendship between the two kings and maybe their lands were closer
in location than we imagine. Guinevere's origins are vague, to say
the least, despite the links with the Gwenhwyvaer of mystical
Welsh legend. Simple conjecture can be part of the pleasure in the
search for Arthur in Somerset. It is part of the magic of a man
whose stories are designed to feed the imagination. But when we try
to discover tangible links we find ourselves in a mysterious maze
which wraps places and people into a pattern of dead ends.

Curiously, close to Queen Camel is a place called Wales, a
reminder of one famous man whose record in history places him
firmly at Queen Camel: the Welshman, Thomas Charles. During his
year-long stay in the village as a curate it is said he suffered a

The Hunting Causeway rose above the marshy
lowlands towards Glastonbury.

meagre salary and loneliness from lack of friends. He was to be
rewarded in his career for when he returned to Wales, he became
another John Wesley, famous for his preaching.

Hunting Causeway

Below Cadbury Castle near the south-west entrance lie the traces of
an old track, part of an ancient causeway which rose above the
marshy lowlands as it made its way to Glastonbury. Once again the

ghostly company of Arthur and his men dominates local legend when on winter nights they are said to ride from the hill and along the causeway to go hunting. Awesome and fearsome some have described the sight as the tips of their lances glow against the night sky and the sound of the hounds are heard eagerly baying. The story reminds one of the age when hunting chiefs pursued their quarry through the Forest of Selwood, at that time a waterlogged terrain which bordered the eastern end of Somerset.

Arthur also figures in the Wild Hunt in French folklore, the *Chasse Artu*. As in many stories of Arthur among the legends of other countries, his image appears positively supernatural. In this case it is like the Valkyrie as they ride the skies. Here, too, Arthur chases through the clouds accompanied by strange and spiritual beings. Sometimes they come down to earth so maybe we can see a connection here with 'Hunting Causeway' as through the years Arthur's fame spread across the seas.

From South Cadbury, secluded and peaceful, with its pretty stone houses, the causeway is said to pass through the two little villages of North and South Barrow. This is the part of Somerset Arthur Mee called 'Caryland'. Cary Moor, its villages Cary Fitzpaine and Babcary and the River Cary, winding from Castle Cary where it rises to the River Parrett. Those who have a sense of the past will wander the quiet lanes and villages of this 'Caryland'. They will see how the indelible mark of man has transformed the once swampy terrain into all the charm and character of rich pastureland where rabbits scuttle into the hedgerows. Somewhere beneath it all lie the remnants of the causeway which Arthur may have used which were traced by a bridlepath until late in the nineteenth century.

At some point the causeway would have crossed the Fosse Way, the old Roman road passing through Ilchester. We can think of Gareth who, determined to earn a knighthood, journeyed to Camelot with two companions. If they traversed the Fosse Way and the causeway across the plain to Cadbury Castle, the words of Tennyson can unfold the scene in our imagination:

> *So when their feet were planted on the plain*
> *that broadened towards the base of Camelot,*
> *Far off, they saw the silver-misty morn*
> *Rolling her smoke about the Royal mount,*
> *That rose between the forest and the field.*

Arthur's Bridge

From Cadbury Castle to Castle Cary the road leads us on to the A371 over the River Brue to Shepton Mallet. Not far from the village of Ditcheat we cross the River Alham over what a sign names as Arthur's Bridge. We are told Arthur needed a crossing here so he built a ford.

Very often named sites are surrounded by the quiet solitude of farming country with its scattered, even remote cottages. Arthur's Bridge is no exception. Here, too, is a place where the river's fast flowing waters feed the pastures growing rich grass for dairy herds. This is an area of Somerset where farms have been known to produce the best cheeses. The naming of the bridge shows the conviction of Somerset people that Arthur *did* come to the county although there will always be those who say it is purely myth represented by reality.

People will always believe that in Somerset Arthur lived, dedicated himself to Christ and the Virgin, fought his greatest battle and his last, then in waters near Glastonbury returned his sword Excalibur. However tenuous the links with Arthur, the variety, shape and mood of places which carry his name, will always stir the imagination, strengthening and keeping alive a belief in his existence.

Ilchester

From Castle Cary to Ilchester we take the road which passes Yeovilton airfield, where the steel Harriers of our modern defence system hover gracefully with nature's sparrowhawks. As we join the old Roman Fosse Way and cross the bridge into the little town it is difficult to realise that for many years it was a place of importance.

Arthur's Bridge 'where the river's fast flowing waters feed the pastures'.

Undistinguished though it may appear today, it provided the perfect defences for a Saxon mint and later in the twelfth century, being the county town of Somerset, it accommodated the county gaol. Here was the seat of Somerset's Assizes where its more unfortunate inmates were housed, locked away on an island at the centre of Ilchester Bridge and, with the many visits from the Sheriff and circuit judges, the prosperity of the town increased. At one time there was a thriving market, at least six parish churches, a Dominican Friary, a Nunnery and seats in Parliament.

The town's decline came with the costly burden of taxation, for the families of those who were hanged had to be supported. King John made sure the walls came down and the Black Death contributed to most of the notable buildings falling into ruin, the remains of which were removed for other building. The quiet side roads now show little of the many years of importance and a colourful past. It is as though the slate has been wiped clean, leaving behind a retired, simple charm.

Ilchester: Archaeologists have discovered
pottery that link this Roman town with the
Arthurian age.

The River Yeo at Ilchester. Could it be the
River Dubglas, site of one of Arthur's battles?

Once, Lindinis was its name and five Roman roads met within its
strong town walls. For the Romans it was an important centre for
local administration. It garrisoned well-drilled soldiers, assisted in
the transportation of lead and was supported by successful farming.
But all too soon the storm clouds gathered, threatening the years of
comparative peace under Roman rule. The day came which saw
worried Britons standing on the seashore losing sight of the sails
which took the legions back to Rome. As the air became still and
hushed, the Saxons threatened like the very few heavy raindrops
which preceed a storm, and the shadow of Arthur began to grow in
the West.

We can have no doubts that the town has its share of secrets
including those from the Dark Ages, the period after the Romans
marched for the last time out through the walls of Lindinis. Life
must have 'gone on' in its own particular Romanized way, coping
with the change in circumstances. Roman coins would still have
slipped from hands and pockets to lie lost in the ground until found
in the gardens of the future. We know little of those times and
depend on the chinks of light revealed by the excavators' tools. It is
from recent discoveries of pieces of pottery that we now know trade
continued with the Mediterranean through to the seventh century.
In the search for the *real* Arthur, we can compare these finds to
those found on the site of the Celtic monastery at Tintagel, for from
the dating of the pottery it is known to have existed during the
Arthurian age.

Explorers of the realm of Arthur in real history now add Ilchester
to their list of conjectured sites, but to imagine that anywhere in
Somerset was once touched by the man is not unreasonable. Real or
romantic, exploration of the greatest enigma in history continues as
it has done for centuries. For some it is like the Quest of the Holy
Grail, a search through a wilderness of symbolism, a private
adventure full of the pitfalls of paradox, yet perhaps leading to
some kind of attainment. We can stand on Ilchester Bridge and
watch the water of the Yeo flow on to meander into the rich plain

beyond. Some have believed this to be the River Dubglas, the site of one of Arthur's battles, described in the ninth-century works of Nennius as being in the region of Linnuis.

Displayed in Ilchester Town Hall is the head-piece of a thirteenth-century mace in which are set three kings and an angel. An inscription reads: *I am a mark of amity; do not forget me.* Although made centuries after Arthur's time, we can liken this statement to the Knights of the Round Table, the symbolism of brotherhood, for in all certainty, we have not forgotten them.

Langport

Westward from Ilchester we come to Langport and here we can turn to Welsh legend and the *Black Book of Carmarthen.* Some say it was here the battle of Llongborth took place, where the leader Gerrans or 'Geraint the Great' was killed, as 'Arthur's brave men who cut with steel' fought alongside him. It is another tenuous link perhaps, but Welsh legend contains many colourful stories of Arthur.

Throughout the country we find the oldest Arthurian legends are Celtic, a strong influence which rises to lie richly on the surface of later literature. The most ancient stories of Arthur were first written in the Welsh poems, based on a long tradition of verbal tellings and blended by Bardic imagination. Arthur is portrayed as a superhuman hero, a warrior, joined by his knights and the images of other familiar characters, in the more primitive adventures of a Tolkien quality. In the poem *Culhwch and Olwen*, we are told how Arthur obtains his sword in an Otherworld named as Ireland.

Langport—perhaps the site of the battle of Llongborth where Geraint the Great was killed.

58

**Stained-glass windows in Langport Church.
Joseph of Arimathea (above) is holding the
cruets said to contain the blood and sweat of
Christ.**

In the Triads, which are compositions grouped in threes, where each one reminds us of another, we are treated to the interwoven plots involving Medrawt (Mordred), Gwalchmei (Gawain) and Drystan (Tristan). Here the Welsh Drystan is one of the 'Three Mighty Swineherds' guarding the swine of March, the King Mark of later stories.

We cannot be sure where the site of the battle would have been but we can see Joseph of Arimathea, the saint who provides a link with Arthur. He is pictured in the beautiful east window of Langport Church, carrying two holy vessels. It is said these contained the blood and sweat of Christ which he brought to Glastonbury along with the beginnings of Christianity. But Joseph is believed to have brought another relic: the vessel used by Christ at the Last Supper, the Holy Grail. As Christ was dying on the cross Joseph caught his blood in the Grail and carried it on his long journey to Glastonbury where he buried it somewhere near the Chalice Well. The red stained waters of the well forever symbolise this legend.

We see the Grail-seeking knights of Arthur embarking on a search which can only be successful through purity in thought and deed. Eventually it was to be Lancelot's son Galahad who achieved the Quest, as the flock of angels carried him away in their midst. The spiritual aura surrounding the Grail is like that of a church to which we are *all* drawn. Each one of us has a different purpose for being here, some deeply personal. Perhaps we should consider just how many will achieve purity and fulfilment from a holy place which holds its own special kind of symbolism and power.

Dunster

Our search for Arthur now takes us further westward and beyond Bridgwater. We can glimpse the Bristol Channel as we follow the folds of the coastline below the rolling Quantock Hills. Beyond lie

The yarn market at Dunster.

Carhampton Church and the coastline where St
Carannog's altar landed.

the Brendon Hills above Dunster and the wild beauty of the vast high moorlands of Exmoor. This is dramatic Arthurian country and we can be forgiven for feeling we are in another world, a landscape far removed from the rest of the county. Today, we can still agree with the words of Collinson, the eighteenth-century parson-historian when he said of the countryside around Dunster: 'This mountainous country may be called the Alps of Somersetshire, the whole country being a picturesque assemblage of lofty hills succeeding each other, with deep romantic vallies winding between them.'

As we view Dunster from the main road to Minehead, the medieval towers and battlements of its castle rise above the trees on the hill like the fairy-tale palaces of Arthurian romance. It is no wonder Somerset is a county steeped in legend, full of visible sites which fire the imagination. Dunster's broad picturesque high street with the castle at one end and covered yarn market at the other, is a fascinating mixture of distinctive charm and whimsical knick-knacks, constantly favoured by its many tourists. But before the days of medieval glory which produced its buildings, we can picture a wilder scene when the Brendon Hills' thickly wooded slopes met marshland before cliffs and a rocky foreshore entered the Severn Sea. This is how it would have been in the days when Arthur is said to have shared the ruling of the region with another Chieftain called Cadwy.

Again Welsh legend comes to the fore, this time in the lives of the saints. In the Life of St Carannog we hear how the saint floated a small altar from Wales across the Bristol Channel. Wherever it

landed would be where he would set up his oratory. When he arrived on the Somerset coast, he met Arthur and asked him if he had seen his altar, telling him why he was there. Arthur *had* found it and tried to use it as a table but everything he put on it mysteriously fell off. He would only return the altar if the saint fulfilled a promise. Arthur demanded the holy man use his powers to banish a dragon which was terrorising the villages of Carhampton and Cleeve. The saint agreed, calling the creature up from the sea and miraculously changing it into a tame and docile creature which goes peaceably on its way.

Here we see the traces of a different side to the character of Arthur which saintly Welsh legend frequently portrays. He is harder, more calculating and drives a hard bargain. He is often shown in a poor light, even tyrannical. This may indicate a legendary man's near mystical abilities not being fully accepted by orthodox thinking in the writings of a later age. But our story does have a happy ending for the benevolent Arthur returns giving the saint, in gratitude for his help, the land for his oratory called Carrum—a place among rocks—now called Carhampton. The Chapel of St Carannog stood and served its purpose until the sixteenth century. Today the site lies under the garden of the former vicarage, east of the present church of St John the Baptist.

The dragon, we know, went on its way and in time became likened to the Minehead hobby horse in the May Day festivities which visits Dunster Castle and a place called Dragon's Cross. In his true form it may be him we see in a carving in Cleeve Church.

Brent Knoll

Like the stories of Arthur, Somerset is composed of enchanting ingredients. Rising out of the coastal plain near Burnham-on-Sea is a curiously lonely hill watching silently over the driving millions on

Brent Knoll — an image from the past.

the motorway. As we travel north from Bridgwater we can see this inescapable landmark coming nearer until invitingly it stands above us. It is the green and noble Brent Knoll which the Romans named *Mons Ranarum*—the Mount of Frogs.

Only by climbing Brent Knoll can its full glory be appreciated. The ancient name conjures up an even more solitary, more hostile image from the past when it was surrounded with vast tracts of marshland covered at times in swirling waters. The hillfort on its summit shows that ancient peoples had found the benefits of this magnificent look-out post long before the Romans.

Did Arthur come here? Local legend says that he did. Inland, between the ranks of the Mendip and Polden Hills, lies the Vale of Avalon stretching towards the distinct form of Glastonbury Tor. Seaward in the Bristol Channel lie the islets of Steep Holm and Flat Holm and the far, blue-grey horizon of the Welsh coastline. We can even look back on our journey to the hazy outline of the distant hills above Dunster. Here we can see *and* be seen, for it was in these high places that beacons were lit as signals in the past.

Brent Knoll — an inescapable landmark coming nearer on the motorway.

We can remember this hill as the scene of a great tragedy in Arthur's life—one he would never forget. When Arthur tested his knights for valour, their task was always undertaken willingly. To stamp out oppression and bring peace to the realm was Arthur's main objective but if a knight perished in an attempt, Arthur always found it hard to accept. At Brent Knoll he learned the task he had set was too much to ask.

While celebrating the Feast of Nativity at Caerleon in Wales he knighted a young price called Yder. Arthur charged him with the test of going ahead on their journey back to Camelot to slay three giants who lived on Brent Knoll and preyed on passers-by. Yder accepted bravely, eager to show his prowess. Three against one was a fearful undertaking and when Arthur arrived with the rest of his knights they found the giants slain, but the young prince also lay dead among them. Overcome with great sorrow, Arthur took his body to Yniswitrin, the name for Glastonbury, where he was solemnly buried by the monks. So great was his remorse he gave the monks the lands of Brent Knoll and the surrounding marshes.

Legend is always given colour in the years of telling. We are told Arthur also gave the monks precious chalices and other items for their use. At one time digging revealed an ancient cuirass resembling Roman craftsmanship but we cannot be sure of its connection. We can be sure, however, this place belonged to the monks, for history confirms this valuable holding once joined the great Glastonbury Abbey estates to the sea.

Dolebury

From Brent Knoll we follow the A38 over the motorway towards the imposing range of the Mendips and enter the pass between the hill's main massif and the lower western reaches to the sea. Steeply inclined and wooded, the pass of grey limestone towers above us on either side as the road bends round the lower slopes of Dolebury hillfort. It is not too difficult to climb this hillfort for, under the care of The National Trust, well-constructed steps aid us upward through clusters of wild violets to the summit. Impressively it overlooks the northern moorlands of Somerset, a landscape where

the present-day boundaries of Avon have no meaning for the purpose of our journey.

Why come to Dolebury hillfort?

Because of its strength of character. Its defences are remarkable and exciting. Grass-clean tumbled banks of stone edge the topmost rampart, the remains of massive walls which once surrounded the twenty-acre plateau. We can look over the moorland to Clevedon, Weston-super-Mare, Brean Down and on even to the distant line of Exmoor. Some days we can watch dark clouds sweeping in from the sea, their curtains of rain moving across a landscape of changing hues. The vision is dramatic, evoking a sense of the past where the full force of the hill, its purpose for outlook and defence, becomes apparent. People, here, may have watched Roman galleys arrive at the mouth of the Axe, or later in a dark Arthurian age seen the Saxons creeping northwards up the coastline.

Dolebury so easily offers itself to be included in our journey for no leader would have ignored the defensive advantages of Mendip's massive range with its vantage points looking to the north and

Dolebury hillfort on the Mendips. 'The vision is
dramatic . . . the full force of the hill for
outlook and defence becomes apparent . . .'

south of Somerset. Like many hillforts Dolebury's character contains an intrinsic air of mystery but, coupled with its position of dominance, is an all too familiar reminder of the image of Arthur. It is a place where we can believe that Arthur lived—and lives.

Congresbury

From the top of Dolebury we can look down its sheer slope on one side, to where the tiny village of Rowberrow secretes itself in a wooded valley. Across the moorland view lies Congresbury, sitting on the banks of the River Yeo. Like Glastonbury, Congresbury may have seen the beginnings of Christianity for we are told St Congar, a sixth-century Celtic missionary, was buried there. Like Joseph of Arimathea, he too is said to have planted his staff in the ground, but in this case it sprouted a yew tree.

Not far from Congresbury is another Cadbury, Cadbury-Congresbury as archaeologists call it, a small fort once occupied by the Romans. Again we cross the path in the search for the real Arthur where academics sort the scripts and sift the soil. As in Ilchester, Tintagel type pottery has been found here pointing to an Arthurian presence.

Always Arthur is a haunting mystery, flitting through the words of almost equally elusive writers. He lies disguised in our landscape among the remains of unrecorded beginnings. For many years heads have been scratched and conclusions proffered. Not surprising are the words once uttered by one of our modern-day 'Chieftains', Sir Winston Churchill, when probably with a familiar 'growl', we are told he said: 'This is not much to show after so much toil and learning!'

Although fragments found from the past are but scraps, they

The Author at Cadbury-Congresbury: 'Always Arthur is a haunting mystery . . .'

provide the chinks of light we need to see into the shadows. The search will go on for an Arthur we can add to the pages of real history, like the great man whose ancestral home lies beneath Dolebury in the village of Churchill. We may then be able to remember them both as striving with others to protect their country and its people.

Cadbury Camp, Tickenham, where Arthur is said to lie sleeping in a cave.

Cadbury Camp

High on the northernmost ridge of Somerset near Clevedon, where the noisy motorway carves its way through to Bristol, we find ourselves at a third Cadbury, We can understand why Somerset is thick with local Arthurian legend. As its title suggests, Cadbury Camp is much smaller than its namesake Cadbury Castle in the south but here again Arthur is said to lie sleeping in a cave. If we shout his name loud enough, he will wake and ride from the hillside with his men.

The hillforts of Somerset are always exciting: powerful atmospheres which seep from the past. Cadbury Camp is different though. It evokes the feeling of happy days full of memories while the drama as always lies in the landscape views. Riders canter by, enjoying with their horses the pleasures they have found, while in a field nearby a curious lonely old wagon contemplates the view north over the Gordano valley.

There is a peace here, high above the activities of modern living below. It is one we can enjoy for a while among the gentle ramparts and sheltering trees. Like Dolebury, here too the National Trust protects a piece of British history from the ravages of a modern kind of onslaught.

Bath—Badon

Arthur lives in many corners of Somerset. Whether a hero of legend or *dux bellorum*, the leader of battles and a conqueror of the Saxon English, he continues to enrich our lives, our desires, even our necessities. Near Bath we can recall a dark time in history when the Saxon onslaught swept across southern Britain. Intent on breaking into the Westcountry, they cunningly sneaked round to the Bristol Channel, taking the British by surprise. They were halted near Bath where they had to face a ferocious attack delivered by the Britons who were led by a mighty leader.

**Solsbury Hill — a strong contender for the
Battle of Badon.**

Little Solsbury hillfort above Batheaston close to Bath has long
been a strong contender for the site of the Battle of Badon. Local
legend tells us the battle lasted three days. Some say Arthur forced
the enemy to take their stand on Bannerdown across the nearby
valley. Despite a strong rear-guard action by the Saxons, with the
aid of Excalibur Arthur mercilessly drove them over the terrain and
up on to Solsbury Hill leaving hundreds in his wake lying dead.
Despite taking refuge in the hillfort, Arthur and his sword finally
overwhelmed them.

The hill being close to Bath is fitting in site and name and we can
still see scattered in the grass the stones which once formed the
walls of the hillfort. Unfortunately the place names of ancient
chronicle have always been vague in their whereabouts and remain a
matter for fervent debate. In searching for an Arthur of real history,
we can begin with the writings of Gildas a sixth-century monk and
contemporary of Arthur's. But this infuriating man, through

prejudice and a disgruntled nature, refrained from naming a victor of any battle. He saw the Saxon invasion as a judgement from God for degenerate govenment of the country. Yet, as if deliberately to throw into confusion the historian of the future, he gives a name for what he calls the 'siege' of *Mons Badonicus*, the hill near Badon. His pen favours Ambrosius Aurelianus but what position he held is as much an enigma for the historians as is Arthur's very existence.

Arthur appears two hundred years later when the monk Nennius extols his name as *dux bellorum*, victor of twelve battles, saying: 'The twelfth battle was on Mount Badon in which nine hundred and sixty men fell in one day from one charge by Arthur and no-one overthrew them except himself alone.'

These words introduced the Arthur of legend into the world of fact. The problem is, he is still clothed in superhuman powers and we have no way of knowing whether he was only an addition of fancy. The works of Nennius fed the minds of twelfth-century historians, William of Malmesbury and Geoffrey of Monmouth. Their writings became interwoven with legend, sowing seeds which flowered in the works of Malory and Tennyson. Eventually, tinged with the colour of local lore, many stories of Arthur were associated with sites in our countryside.

Today, many scholars, including historians, conduct exhaustive researches into the reality of Arthur. The results prove only a probability, so Arthur still remains the chief myth of Britain. On *our* journey in the search for a real Arthur at Bath, we can explore a new dimension, that of psycho-expansion through which a lady, already introduced by Michael Williams, believes she was King Arthur in a previous life. We can tread the paths of official history accompanied by the strange presence of mythology and we can also listen to a person who takes a more unorthodox route. For her it is a remarkable experience while for us it presents the images of another probable truth, that of the cold reality of war in ancient history. It is evident what the lady sees in her regression is *very* real.

'You ask: "Was I at the Battle of Badon and was it at Bath?" Yes, I *was* at the battle and things had been altering in my life up to that point. I had a heightened awareness and great physical strength. But I can't bring myself to view the battle, it is too much, the experiences are so horrific. If I do attempt it, I am completely drained, utterly exhausted. When I first had this experience, I received a great deal of help from my "company" who were dealing with the fourth dimension, spiritually "tuning-in" with each other and myself to bolster the strength of the physical body.'

We can see the battle for her is the ultimate in nightmares with the positions reversed—as Arthur she is the pursuer. The lady goes on.

'I was amazed to see an equilateral cross upon the backs of many of those around me and upon myself. Interestingly the cross was on my back *and* my front and each had in their centre a red crystal—it certainly had a great deal to do with having extra power. This may seem very fictional and extraordinary but it was an extraordinary battle. The terrain, I felt, was east of Bath. In this life Bath has an enormous "pull" for me but not within the confines of the city. I feel, too, Badon was in Wiltshire . . . I can see the terrain very clearly. There is a good deal of talk going on and how the strategy should be. It is all *very* complicated. It is amazing how these men have an immense sense of awareness. How can I describe it? You can liken it to the Red Indians, the way they used sense, sight and sound, a "tuning-in" to the earth . . . yes, the area of Bath, the Wiltshire side, that was Badon.'

The lady goes on to say she knew Ambrosius, the Roman.

'You see, he was to me a "father" figure. He taught me all the preliminary strategy of battle in my early years from a time when I was a very tiny child. He gave me my first weapon, what seemed to me to be a small sword—probably a dagger. He taught and gave me the knowledge I would need to be a soldier, the many Roman ideas of battle, the forming of lines, positions, use of the terrain. Battle was not a very jolly kind of skirmish I can tell you for an absolute certainty. The things we wore, the paraphernalia which went with the different strategies was amazing. It was the habit to use axes when you got older and I am sure of that because this man Arthur was absolutely "spot-on" with the axe. He could cut a blade of grass in two with it at a distance! When I come out of an experience, I often ask myself practical questions like, whatever happened to all those axes, all those weapons. It is *ghastly* to view. You have never seen anything like it. Nuclear war is clean compared to that! Ambrosius was in the right-place at the right time to teach Arthur extraordinary physical feats. Arthur, in a sense was used for these purposes but it had to be. I also know Ambrosius lives. To this day he is still concerned with terrain and exploration.'

Some may scoff at this encounter on our journey and some may even wish to know more. No-one can deny its fascination or that it would take this lady's lifetime to relive every detail of her life as Arthur.

From Little Solsbury Hill we can look down on the lovely city of Bath, the Roman Aquae Sulis. At the time of the Battle of Badon it lay abandoned and ruined in a swampy valley. Thankfully we cannot hear the terrifying echo of steel from the past . . . but there was a time when it was not unknown for people to gather cap-fulls of teeth from Bannerdown.

It was probably some fifty years after the Battle of Badon that the Saxons swept once more into the Westcountry, finally splitting the British kingdoms. In 577, at Dyrham Park near Bath, three British kings were killed by the Saxon King Ceawlin. Arthur's name was not among them. Although Bath was taken along with Gloucester and Cirencester, it was to be another 81 years before central Somerset was conquered.

Arthur's Point

Turning south again towards the heartland of Somerset and the Mendip Hills, we find a promontory overlooking Wookey Hole caves. This is Arthur's Point, a perfect look-out post from where he could scan the Vale of Avalon to the sea. Here, local legend says, he pondered and plotted the downfall of the Witch of Wookey, enlisting the help of a Glastonbury monk to turn her into stone. This story reminds us of the Welsh tale of Culhwch and Olwen, where the Black Hag is a witch whose blood Arthur seeks.

Merlin, the wizard, is the focus for many of the supernatural qualities which surround Arthur in the stories and Mendips' caves can remind us of the enchanter's rapid exit from the scene. Prophet he was and, although not able to forsee his own folly, his magic influenced Arthur's whole life. When Geoffrey of Monmouth introduced Merlin in his historical writings as the mystical shape-changer and instigator of the birth of Arthur, the magician became as much a source for inventive writing in the future as Arthur was.

Shape-changer he still is, for he has become like Arthur a perennial character. In Tolkien he is Gandalf, a wise and powerful magician, while modern films add more amusing interpretations of the personality. Like Arthur, Merlin lives on, weaving a magic in people's minds.

As we stand on Arthur's Point we can sense the changes in the countryside if we view them in the light of legend. Lift the veil of the modern landscape and we can see below in our imagination a peaceful mixture of marshy expanses and muddy pools, dense woods and fertile fields. Among the hills, Glastonbury Tor towers supreme. Perhaps from his Point, Arthur anguished over his Queen for the Tor was the stronghold of King Melwas, ruler of the 'Summerland'. Melwas kidnapped the Queen, holding her captive on the Tor. Arthur's power in the Westcountry was such that he gathered many men from Devon and Cornwall to rescue her and arrived ready to do battle. Bloodshed was averted when St Gildas

Arthur's Point from where Arthur could scan the Vale of Avalon.

and the Abbot of Glastonbury convinced Melwas no good could come by his actions. A treaty was negotiated and Arthur regained his Queen.

Once again local legend has evolved from Welsh origins, where Merlin appears as Myrddin, a wild and mysterious wizard who comes from the north. The abduction of Guinevere comes from The Life of St Gildas written in the twelfth century by Caradoc of Llancarfan, while we can remember how in Malory's later version it was a knight called Meleagaunt who carries her off.

Beckery

As we approach Glastonbury, the Isle of Avalon, we are guided by its compelling and dramatic landmark, the Tor. Few have not been inspired by its presence for the curious emerald green form emits a

Queen Guinevere who shared a forbidden love
with Arthur's most courtly knight, Lancelot.

mysticism which is hard to define. This crowning glory of
Glastonbury is not alone for it looks over domed Chalice Hill,
Windmill Hill and the long ridge of Wearyall Hill to the west.

Beneath Wearyall Hill on the edge of the moors lies the little
village of Beckery swamped by the progress of industry. Its past is
hidden but it has been touched by the magic of Arthur. At one time
it was a simple green knoll, a low island among the marshes and a
wide glistening mere—traditionally a holy place, its chapel a shrine
dedicated to St Mary Magdalene.

Adapted from one of the Grail stories, legend tells of how Arthur
was sleeping as a guest at the Convent of St Peter on Wearyall Hill.
He dreamed three times of an Angel who commanded him to go to
the Chapel of St Mary Magdalene at Beckery. Telling his servant he
would go if it happened again, the inquisitive man crept out the next
night while Arthur was sleeping and went to the chapel. Inside, a

Beckery — its past is hidden by progress.

man's body lay on a bier with four tapers burning at each corner. In their light gold candlesticks gleamed on the altar prompting the greedy servant to steal one and flee. Unfortunately someone stepped from the shadows and stabbed him in the groin. He crawled back to Arthur and, before dying, confessed what he had done.

When Arthur arrived at the chapel, a priest was preparing for mass. Arthur prayed long and hard. Suddenly a great light filled the chapel and in its midst the Virgin Mary appeared carrying her son. To Arthur's surprise, the priest offered him, instead of the host, the body of the child which he consumed and afterwards saw miraculously appear whole again on the altar. The Virgin then gave Arthur a crystal cross before she vanished with her son.

Maybe this legend portrays a time in Arthur's life when he needed to renounce any remaining allegiance he may have had to pagan gods. We read of him vowing a lifetime of service to the Virgin and her Son and carrying their image on his shoulders into battle.

Pomparles Bridge—the Bridge Perilous

Flooded levels — '. . . an aqueous and oozy terrain'.

Excalibur & Pomparles Bridge

It is only a short walk from Beckery to the end of Wearyall Hill where unimpressive Pomparles Bridge—the Bridge Perilous—spans the River Brue. Far from romantic, it carries the traffic which pounds along the busy road from Glastonbury to Bridgwater.

Leland, the historian, wrote in Tudor times of 'a Bridge of Stone of four Arches communely caullid Pontperlus where men fable that Arture cast his Swerd'. Sir John Harington said in the sixteenth century that Arthur was transported away in a barge 'from a bridge called Pomperles, near the said Glassenbury, and so conveyed by unknown persons with promise to bring him back again one day'.

Here we see how the power of Arthur's eternal appeal has been fused into the landscape, adding another variation to a familiar sequence of events: a belief that it was Arthur *himself* who, despite his terrible wound, staggered to the bridge and with one mighty effort hurled Excalibur into the Brue.

Excalibur, Arthur's constant companion and magical source for power and strength in battle, had to be returned to the Lady of the

A barge of lamenting Queens bore Arthur away
to the 'island valley of Avilion'.

Lake, for Arthur alone had been chosen to have possession of it. As
with the Holy Grail, there is a symbolism behind the gift of the
sword. It can be seen as a personal instrument for advancement
towards perfection. In different ways we can be chosen and
presented with opportunities on the path of life. If the means we are
given are used wisely and responsibly, we may find in the end
complete achievement. In a sense, with Excalibur, Arthur *was*
successful but he failed with the scabbard by neglecting it and
losing it forever.

Helped by the expanse of moorland which stretches into the Vale
of Avalon, it is not too difficult to visualise what this place was like
in Arthur's time. We can see how the river waters would have once
spread in a wide lake over the marshes. Near to the present road
towards Street was a Roman causeway of wood and stone above a
bog. From Street a Roman road led the way on higher ground to
Somerton, Ilchester and on towards Cadbury Castle. We travel this
route today with comparative ease but how would it have been for
Arthur when his closest companions carried him from the Battle of
Camlann?

We cannot forget that final dramatic scene when in Tennyson's
words, '. . . because his wound was deep. The bold Sir Bedivere
uplifted him, and bore him to a chapel . . .' Then the all important
command '. . . take Excalibur, and fling him far into the middle mere
. . .' We remember the not so bold Bedivere's reluctance to do as he
was bid, until at the third request he saw the arm rise from the
waters 'clothed in white samite, mystic, wonderful' to receive
Excalibur. As the barge of lamenting Queens bore Arthur away to
the 'island-valley of Avilion', the sad and solitary figure of Sir
Bedivere . . .

> thought he saw, the speck that bare the King,
> Down that long water opening on the deep
> Somewhere far off, pass on and on, and go
> From loss and vanish into light.

**The Chalice Well at Glastonbury where perhaps
the Grail is buried.**

Glastonbury—The Isle of Avalon

It is an island of dreams, a magical place of legend, mystery and imagination. Glastonbury can be many things to many people but for the pilgrim drawn by the mistique of the name of Avalon it is the resting place of King Arthur.

Imaginations in the past could not resist being inspired by the island which rose from marsh and swamp in a cluster of green hills, among them the curious conical Tor. The Welsh called it *Ynyswitrin*, the 'glass-island', a mythological Otherworld. Geoffrey of Monmouth connected the name Avalon to the Welsh for 'apple' and tells of Arthur's sword being forged at Avalon and how the wounded King is taken by the Wizard Taliesin to the 'Isle of Apples' an idyllic land of plenty. The island is ruled by nine sisters, one of them Morgen, an enchantress and healer. She lays Arthur on a golden couch and promises to cure him if he stays with her. This is the Morgen we see depicted much later in the medieval tales of Malory as the less than benign Morgan le Fay, Arthur's half-sister.

Among the ruins of the Abbey we can look at the marked grave where once the tomb of Arthur stood before the High Altar and be acutely conscious of a numinous power which lies in the surrounding massive ancient stones. Near the great walls of the ruined Chapels of St Joseph and St Mary which stand open to the skies, is the site of a once smaller, more humble chapel. We cannot be certain whether it was built by Joseph of Arimathea when he visited Glastonbury but we do know the chapel *was* there. The historian William of Malmesbury described it in the twelfth century as: 'The Old Chapel of our Lady of Glastonbury . . . It was at first formed of wattles, and from the beginning breathed and was redolent of a mysterious divine sanctity, which spread throughout the country . . . It was so holy.'

Glastonbury has remained, above all things, a place of great holiness, sacred in the hearts of people who believe it to be England's cradle of Christianity and the resting place of St Patrick and St Joseph. It is a delicate mixture of legend and history which has been woven together to give us the stories of Joseph of Arimathea. They tell of his coming long before Arthur's time and building the little chapel of wattles now believed to be the first Christian church in the country. We can see the Holy Thorns, the children of Joseph's staff which he planted on Wearyall Hill and which bloom at Christmas. We hear how, along with Christianity, he brought a chalice or Grail containing the blood of Christ. Like Arthur's Knights, there are still the 'Grail-seekers', some of whom believe it is buried somewhere in Chalice Hill or Chalice Well below the Tor.

Many people maintain Glastonbury to be a mystical centre, a place to feel potent vibrations, the remnants of a strong magic from ancient pagan belief. Deeply rooted in the landscape, the energies of past rituals of a different kind of worship are believed to filter through the atmosphere, creating a powerful harmony in balance with the rhythms of nature. Maybe the sacred Seers of long ago did practice a more mysterious form of enlightenment and harnessed the elemental forces of earth and heaven, man and the cosmos. The ritual importance of the Tor lies deep in ancient belief together with the strange meaning of the maze in its spiralling ramparts. It is here, many say, the vibrations are strongest and it has become a focal point for many a spiritual seeker.

Linked to the Tor is another mystery, the Glastonbury Zodiac, a ten-mile-wide circle of terrestrial figures formed by features in the landscape and unseen from the ground. Can we possibly believe this Zodiac has an Arthurian connection? Katherine Maltwood, its discoverer, thought so, for in the 1920s she followed the Quest of King Arthur's Knights in their search for the Holy Grail on an Ordnance Survey map. As the patterns emerged, she claimed the Zodiac to be the original Round Table with the seated figures of King Arthur, Guinevere, Merlin and the Knights. Arthur is described in the shape of Sagittarius, and depicts the disturbing dream he had in Malory's *Morte d'Arthur* just before the Battle of Camlann. Clothed in gold and made 'fast to a wheel', Arthur is 'up-so-down' and threatened 'by all manner of serpents and worms'. In the Zodiac he is a Sun-King hanging upside-down on a wheel, attacked by Scorpio and the Piscean Leviathan. His horse is the Pennard Hills with Arthur's Bridge on its tail and Pennard is said to mean Arddier's Hill-top. His body is the Baltonsborough plain, a

Glastonbury Tor: 'a compelling and dramatic landmark'.

name connected with the sun-god Baal. His leg drops into the horn of Capricorn formed by the earthwork Ponter's Ball, known by some as the Golden Coffin. Capricorn can be likened to the mysterious White Hart, hunted in folklore and symbolised as a creature of secret knowledge. Here, we are told, is Merlin who in his ancient wisdom made the Round Table through which the Grail Quest began. The Aquarian effigy is set around Glastonbury in an older form of the Phoenix, the symbol for rejuvenation. In its midst the Tor becomes again the instrument for a strange power, its paths forming the way to the hidden symbolism of the Grail.

At Glastonbury beliefs are challenged, mysteries deepen, and none more so than the finding of Arthur's grave. On our journey we have followed a shadow taking many forms but at Glastonbury we are presented with a reality in history which at first glance gives the shadow some substance.

On the advice of an old British bard, Henry II suggested to the monks of the Abbey that Arthur's grave might be there. In 1191 while digging in their own burial ground south of the Lady Chapel

they found a large stone seven feet down bearing on its underside a lead cross. A Latin inscription on the cross said 'Here lies buried the renowned King Arthur in the Isle of Avalon'. Digging a further nine feet the monks found a coffin, a hollowed-out tree trunk of oak and inside were the bones of a man. He was large in stature and his skull bore the evidence of ten blows, one of which must have been so damaging as to cause his death. In the same coffin were the bones of a smaller person and a lock of yellow hair which crumbled when touched. These bones had to be Guinevere. Eventually, in 1278 on the 12 April, Edward I and his Queen Eleanor saw the bones wrapped in silken cloth and placed in a marble tomb in front of the High Altar of the Abbey church. During the Dissolution the abbey was pillaged and the tomb desecrated, but the cross appears to have survived until the early seventeenth century when William Camden published a drawing of it. Afterwards it mysteriously disappeared.

How can we view this grave of Arthur's? Some may see it as Malory describes. After Arthur had been borne away in the barge, Bedivere discovers a hermit pouring over a grave in a chapel near Glastonbury. Bedivere is told '. . . at midnight, here came a number of ladies and brought hither a dead corpse, and prayed me to bury him . . .' Although the hermit cannot give the name of the corpse, Bedivere believes it is the body of Arthur and thereafter commits his life to prayer. We then hear of how Guinevere was brought to Glastonbury after dying at Amesbury where she became a nun. Others may believe the finding of the grave was purely a publicity stunt, at a time when the Abbey was being rebuilt after the great fire in 1184. Then there are those who regard the passing of Arthur as having a more mystical meaning, for a grave may not have existed. Perhaps we should also consider the relationship Arthur appeared to have with the monks. His character did not always live up to the ideals of the clergy, so how did he qualify to be buried at the Abbey?

We can go on asking questions, following an ideal or simply reading the stories. Along with the words of chronicle, the Welsh poems and the romance of Malory and Tennyson, we can add the thrill of modern thought. These are all the ingredients we have

Arthur's grave at Glastonbury.

carried with us on our journey, our Quest to discover King Arthur in the Somerset countryside. Whatever our beliefs, we have been presented with an all-embracing personality, a supernatural hero who influences real history and wisdom of thought. Somerset can only be a part of the story for an Arthurian ethos continues to spread its magic throughout our land, to the Continent and beyond, stirring millions of hearts everywhere with the presence of an undying King.

The Vale of Avalon

Maybe the song of the bird spirit of a King echoes across the Somerset levels where from damp and boggy ground the rich scent of meadowsweet hangs heavily on the air. Perhaps it flies through this Vale of Avalon with its lush meadows and willow-edged rhines which have emerged with a subtle beauty from the waters and dank impenetrable swamp of the past. Watching over this vista as it stretches to the sea, Glastonbury Tor rises purposefully from the Isle of Avalon. The senses cannot escape its personality. It is extraordinary, an entrancing symbol for the conjuring of dreams.

As in all of Somerset the past remains, revealed through a veneer of modern features, but when thick low lying mist fills the vales, it is then the Avalonian scene presents its most ancient character. The imposing countenance of the Tor rules over islets and islands in a seemingly aqueous and oozy terrain. To such a landscape Arthur came after wild and rugged Cornwall breathed life into him.

The straight and tarmaced roads which cross the vale between green pastures and peat fields were not the first to be laid, for Neolithic man also had his engineering achievements. Embalmed beneath the peat at Shapwick and partly excavated, are the wooden remains of a 6,000-year-old trackway, the Sweet Track. It may have linked the Polden Hills to Westhay when a season of dryness permitted. At one time the villages of Godney and Meare were 'lake villages' where the people lived in mud and wattle huts raised on

**The Vale of Avalon where Glastonbury Tor
rises purposefully.**

stilts, while Wedmore, close to the feet of Mendip, was an island
surrounded by water.

The Vale of Avalon is too lovely to go unexplored. Leave the car
and walk along the rhines, it is an exercise in ground-level
observation. Amphibious floral delights add colour to the dominant
green in the area, with the white and mauve of water violets,
flowering rushes and the gentle hues of comfrey. Bog myrtle, with
its candlelike red berries, grows on the peat, a rare plant once used
for feeding livestock and dyeing wool. There may be a chance to see
the insectivorous great-sundew fasten on a fly while the elongated
shadow of a grey heron flying overhead evokes a prehistoric vision.
Dragonflies, butterflies and beetles love the aquatic abundance
and all year round the characteristic songs of marsh birds compete

across this rich expanse. Lapwing, curlew and snipe joining the warblers, whinchats and wagtails, while mute swans idle away the hours in the waters of the rhines.

Arthur defended a 'Faith', his people *and* their land, a land which he must have surely loved. It is but a small task to protect the legacies which nature leaves us so that we can pass them on with our legends to future generations. They, too, can then find their own special kind of 'magic' in the Vale of Avalon where, in the still of a June night as the summer mists gather for morning across the levels, a nightingale will be heard bursting forth with its impassioned story for its mate.

Or is it the spirit of a King?

ALSO AVAILABLE

KING ARTHUR COUNTRY IN CORNWALL
THE SEARCH FOR THE REAL ARTHUR

by Brenda Duxbury, Michael Williams and Colin Wilson. Over 50 photographs and 3 maps.

An exciting exploration of the Arthurian Sites in Cornwall and Scilly, including the related legends of Tristan and Iseult, with The Search for the Real Arthur by Colin Wilson.

'. . . provides a refreshing slant on an old story linking it with the present.'

Caroline Righton. The Packet Newspapers

SUPERNATURAL IN SOMERSET

by Rosemary Clinch.

Atmospheres, healing, dowsing, fork-bending and strange encounters are only some of the subjects featured inside these pages. A book, destined to entertain and enlighten—one which will trigger discussion—certain to be applauded and attacked.

'. . . may well be the sort of material which will change a cottage industry into an international conglomerate.'

Vernon Hall, West Review

MYSTERIES IN THE SOMERSET LANDSCAPE

by Sally Jones

Sally Jones, in her fourth Bossiney title, travels among the Mysteries in the Somerset Landscape. An intriguing journey among deep mysteries in a 'fascinating and varied landscape.'

'This is a whirlwind package holiday of sorcery and legend, touching down here and there before whizzing off in search of still more fascinating fare.'

Mid Somerset Series of Newspapers

UNKNOWN SOMERSET

by Rosemary Clinch and Michael Williams.

A journey across Somerset, visiting off-the-beaten-track places of interest. Many specially commissioned photographs by Julia Davey add to the spirit of adventure.

'Magical Somerset . . . from ley lines to fork-bending; a journey into the unknown . . . a guide which makes an Ordnance Survey map "an investment in adventure".'

Western Daily Press

THE QUANTOCKS

by Jillian Powell with photographs by Julia Davey

'Seen from Taunton or The Mendips, the Quantocks look timeless . . .' Sensitive combination of words and pictures produce a delightful portrait of the area.

'. . . a charming portrait of an area of great natural beauty and much historic interest.'

Somerset and Avon Life

OFFBEAT SOMERSET

by Dan Lees
Author and journalist, Dan Lees, explores some off-beat stories and characters of Somerset.
'... he has looked at the story behind the story ...'   Somerset & Avon Life

UNKNOWN BRISTOL

by Rosemary Clinch
Introduced by David Foot, this is Bossiney's first Bristol title. 'Rosemary Clinch relishes looking round the corners and under the pavement stones ...'
'... gets into the nooks and crannies of Bristol, England, an ancient and historic city. Rosemary Clinch takes us to the parts of the city that are often missed. She gives insights into the life of the docks and the communities around ...'
                        The Book Exchange, International Monthly Book Review Journal

LEGENDS OF SOMERSET

by Sally Jones. 65 photographs and drawings.
Sally Jones travels across rich legendary landscapes. Words, drawings and photographs all combine to evoke a spirit of adventure.
'On the misty lands of the Somerset plain—as Sally Jones makes clear—history, legend and fantasy are inextricably mixed.'   Dan Lees, The Western Daily Press

WESTCOUNTRY MYSTERIES

Introduced by Colin Wilson
A team of authors probe mysterious happenings in Somerset, Devon and Cornwall. Drawings and photographs all add to the mysterious content.
'A team of authors have joined forces to re-examine and probe various yarns from the puzzling to the tragic.'   James Belsey, Bristol Evening Post

STRANGE SOMERSET STORIES

Introduced by David Foot with chapters by Ray Waddon, Jack Hurley, Lornie Leete-Hodge, Hilary Wreford, David Foot, Rosemary Clinch and Michael Williams.
'Publisher Michael Williams has tried to capture an essence of the Westcountry bizarre ...'   Peter John, Bath and West Evening Chronicle

GHOSTS OF SOMERSET

by Peter Underwood
The President of the Ghost Club completes a hat-trick of hauntings for Bossiney.
'... ghostly encounters that together make up the rich tapestry of the Ghosts of Somerset.'   Western Gazette

We shall be pleased to send you our catalogue giving full details of our growing list of titles for Devon, Cornwall and Somerset and forthcoming publications.

If you have difficulty in obtaining our titles, write direct to Bossiney Books, Land's End, St Teath, Bodmin, Cornwall.